Birds Are Fun!

Mary Elizabeth Salzmann

Consulting Editor, Diane Craig, M.A./Reading Specialist

Sandcastle

An Imprint of Abdo Publishing
abdobooks.com

abdobooks.com

Published by Abdo Publishing, a division of ABDO, PO Box 398166, Minneapolis, Minnesota 55439.

Printed in the United States of America, North Mankato, Minnesota

052021
092021

THIS BOOK CONTAINS RECYCLED MATERIALS

Design: Sarah DeYoung, Mighty Media, Inc.
Production: Mighty Media, Inc.
Cover Photograph: iStockphoto
Interior Photographs: iStockphoto, pp. 4, 13, 17; Shutterstock, pp. 4 (gray parrot), 5, 7, 9, 11, 15, 19, 21, 22

Library of Congress Control Number: 2019957508

Publisher's Cataloging-in-Publication Data
Names: Salzmann, Mary Elizabeth, author.
Title: Birds are fun! / by Mary Elizabeth Salzmann
Description: Minneapolis, Minnesota : Abdo Publishing, 2022 | Series: Pets are fun! | Includes online resources and index
Identifiers: ISBN 9781532193095 (lib. bdg.) | ISBN 9781098211738 (ebook)
Subjects: LCSH: Pets--Juvenile literature. | Birds as pets--Juvenile literature. | Birds--Behavior --Juvenile literature. | Pets--Behavior--Juvenile literature.
Classification: DDC 636.08--dc23

SandCastle™ Level: Emerging

SandCastle™ books are created by a team of professional educators, reading specialists, and content developers around five essential components—phonemic awareness, phonics, vocabulary, text comprehension, and fluency—to assist young readers as they develop reading skills and strategies and increase their general knowledge. All books are written, reviewed, and leveled for guided reading and early reading intervention programs for use in shared, guided, and independent reading and writing activities to support a balanced approach to literacy instruction. The SandCastle™ series has four levels that correspond to early literacy development. The levels are provided to help teachers and parents select appropriate books for young readers.

EMERGING • BEGINNING • TRANSITIONAL • FLUENT

Contents

Birds Are Fun!

Can you find these pet birds in this book?

canary

parrots

lovebird

cockatiel

macaw

parakeet

This bird is young.

This bird is white.

This bird is blue.

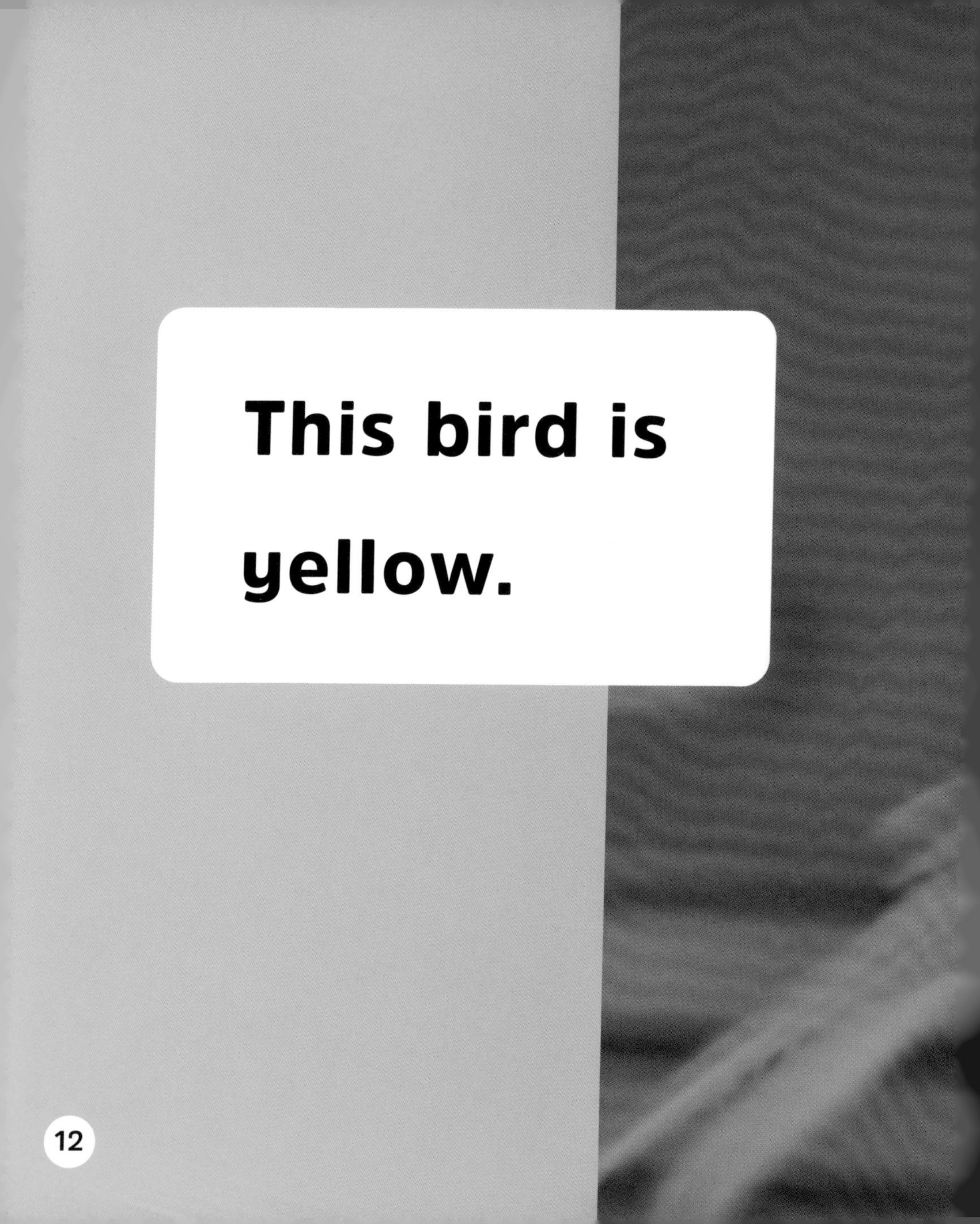

This bird is yellow.

This bird is gray.

This bird is green.

This bird is little.

This bird is big.

What Else Did You See?

ball

boy

girl

plate

Index

Teacher's Guide

ATOS: 0.5 **GRL: A** **Word Count: 32**

High-Frequency Words

big blue is little

this white yellow

Content Words

bird, gray, green, young

Before Reading

- Tell students that the title of the book is *Birds Are Fun!*
- Summarize the content of the book.
- Have students look through the book. Ask them what they see in the pictures.
- Choose a few new vocabulary words. Have students predict what letter each word starts with. Then have them find the words in the book.

After Reading

Ask students questions about the book's content, such as:

- Have you ever held or petted a bird? What was it like?
- Do you have a pet? What kind of pet is it?
- What other animals would you like to read about?